W9-BEK-585

Ben Franklin
and His First Kite

written by
Stephen Krensky

illustrated by
Bert Dodson

Aladdin

New York London Toronto Sydney Singapore

First Aladdin edition June 2002
Text copyright © 2002 by Stephen Krensky
Illustrations copyright © 2002 by Bert Dodson

Aladdin Paperbacks
An imprint of Simon & Schuster
Children's Publishing Division
1230 Avenue of the Americas
New York, NY 10020
All rights reserved, including the right of
reproduction in whole or in part in any form.
READY-TO-READ is a registered trademark of Simon & Schuster, Inc.
CHILDHOOD OF FAMOUS AMERICANS
is a registered trademark of Simon & Schuster, Inc.
The text for this book was set in 18 Point Century Old Style.
Designed by Lisa Vega.
The illustrations were rendered in water color.
Manufactured in the United States of America
8 10 9

Library of Congress Cataloging-in-Publication Data:
Krensky, Stephen.
Ben Franklin and his first kite / written by Stephen Krensky ;
illustrated by Bert Dodson.–1st Aladdin ed.
p. cm.
Summary: Two popular series, Ready-to-Read and Childhood of Famous Americans, combine to present the story of young Ben Franklin who loves doing experiments and cannot wait to test out his latest idea involving a kite!
ISBN-13: 978-0-689-84984-8 (ISBN-10: 0-689-84984-2) (pbk.)
ISBN-13: 978-0-689-84985-5 (ISBN-10: 0-689-84985-0) (library ed.)
[1. Franklin, Benjamin, 1706-1790–Childhood and youth–Juvenile literature.
2. Franklin, Benjamin, 1706-1790–Childhood and youth. 3. Scientists–United States–Biography–Juvenile literature. 4. Inventors–United States–Biography–Juvenile literature.
5. Scientists. 6. Inventors.]
[E]-dc21
2003273907

Ten-year-old Benjamin Franklin
was hard at work
in his father's candle shop.
He was cutting wicks.
He carefully laid out each one.

Ben stretched his arms
and let out a yawn.
Candles could be tall or short,
fat or thin,
and even different colors.
But there was nothing fun
about candles for Ben.

"When do you think
we'll be done today?"
Ben asked his father.
"Soon enough," his father answered.

"Why? Do you have special plans?"
Ben's father smiled.
It was a rare day indeed
when Ben did not have
a plan in mind.

"Yes," said Ben.

"I want to try an experiment
at the millpond."

"You'll be swimming, then?"
his father asked.

Ben grinned. "Partly," he said.

His father nodded.

Ben was a fine swimmer.

HART

That afternoon Ben
flew down the streets of Boston.
He was headed for home.
Along the way he noticed the
waves cresting in the harbor.
The ships rocked back and forth.
That was good, he thought.
He needed a strong wind today.

When Ben got to his house,
his mother met him at the door.
Inside, two of his sisters
were busy making
hasty pudding by the hearth.
Ben had sixteen brothers and sisters.
"Ben," his mother said,
"why are you in such a hurry?"
Ben told her about his plan.

"Since your father approves,
I won't keep you,"
said his mother.
"Just be back for supper."
Ben nodded.
He ran to get the kite
he had made the week before.
Then he left the house.

At the millpond
a few of Ben's friends
had arrived to watch.
"You've picked a poor place
to fly a kite," said one.
Ben shrugged.
"I'm doing an experiment," he said.

Ben got undressed.
He gave his clothes
to one of his friends.
"Please carry these
to the other side
of the pond," he said.
"What are you going to do?"
asked the other boys.
"Carry the kite while you swim?"
"No," said Ben.
"The kite is going
to carry me."

"But that kite's nothing special.
It's just paper, sticks, and string,"
said one boy.
"That's true," Ben said.
"But you see,
the kite isn't the invention.
The invention is what
I'm going to do with it."

Ben raised the kite in the air.
Once the wind had caught
and carried it aloft,
Ben walked into the water.
There he lay on his back, floating.

"I'm going to cross this pond
without swimming a stroke,"
said Ben.

The wind tugged on the kite.
The kite string tightened.
The water began
to ripple at Ben's feet.
The kite was pulling him!

The boys whooped
and hollered as Ben
glided across the pond.
Finally he reached the other side.
The other boys met him there.
"That was amazing!" said one.
"You crossed the whole pond
without swimming a stroke,"
said another.

"What will you do next?"
they asked.
"Another invention?"
"A different experiment?"
Ben didn't know.
But he was sure he would think
of something.

This book is based on a story about Benjamin Franklin. The timeline below identifies important events in his life.

1706	Born on January 17, the fifteenth of seventeen children
1716	Goes to work in his father's chandlery at age 10
1718	Becomes apprentice to his brother James
1723	Runs away from Boston for Philadelphia
1729	Buys the *Pennsylvania Gazette*
1730	Marries Deborah Read (has three children)
1732	Begins to print *Poor Richard's Almanack*
1740	Invents Pennsylvania fireplace, later called Franklin Stove
1752	Flies kite in thunderstorm to show that lightning is a form of electricity
1775	Joins the Second Continental Congress
1776	Helps draft and signs the *Declaration of Independence*
1776	Becomes American representative to France
1783	Helps negotiate Treaty of Paris
1790	Dies in Philadelphia on April 17